NICK OWEN'S

* When were the first Winter Olympics held?

* Who won the 1989 FA Cup?

* How many players are there on each side in a hurling match?

* How many players are in a netball team?

Now is your chance to pit your wits against Nick Owen, ITV's top sports presenter. Featuring all sports, from football to ice-skating.

About the author:

NICK OWEN is married with four children and lives in Berkhamsted, Herts. He attended Shrewsbury School and Leeds University, where he studied Classics, before moving to his first full-time job as a trainee reporter on the *Doncaster Evening Post*. He has worked in radio and television sport since 1973, with a three-year break to present breakfast television at TV-am in the early 1980s. He returned to ITV Sport in 1986. He is a sports fanatic, and loves playing squash and golf in his spare time.

NICK OWEN'S SPORTS QUIZ

Compiled by Nick Owen
and Sandy Ransford

Illustrated by Ian McGill

KNIGHT BOOKS
Hodder and Stoughton

First published in Great Britain in
1990 by Knight Books

The rights of Nick Owen to be identi-
fied as the author of the text of this
work and of Ian McGill to be identi-
fied as the illustrator of this work
have been asserted by them in
accordance with the Copyright,
Designs and Patents Act 1988.

Photoset by Rowland Phototype-
setting Ltd., Bury St Edmunds,
Suffolk. Printed and bound in Great
Britain for Hodder and Stoughton
Children's Books, a division of
Hodder and Stoughton Ltd., Mill
Road, Dunton Green, Sevenoaks,
Kent, TN13 2YA (Editorial Office:
47 Bedford Square, London WC1B
3DP) by Cox & Wyman Ltd., Reading
Berks.

British Library C.I.P.

Owen, Nick
  Nick Owen's sports quiz.
  1. Sports
  I. Title II. Ransford, Sandy
796

ISBN 0-340-52093-0

Foreword

I remember, when I was a youngster, having a friend to stay and my father complaining of the noise long after bedtime as our intermittent shouts rent the night air:

'Rod Laver!'
'Crewe Alexandra!'
'Mary Rand!'
'Aston Villa!'

It was quiz time, of course, and that friend has since become a leading TV sports producer at the BBC, while I talk about my great passion on ITV. The point is, though, that youngsters love a quiz, and I have great fun today testing my children with the knowledge gleaned over many years from my hobby, which is now also my job. Aren't I lucky?

Sandy Ransford and I have tried to make the questions as varied and interesting as possible with a wide selection of categories, some considerably more difficult than others. I hope the book gives you lots of fun, and helps you to learn about the subject that joins the world in friendship, regardless of race or religion. But don't keep your father or your mother awake late at night!

Contents

Firsts

1. Who was the first man to run a mile in under four minutes?
2. What happened for the first time in a Wembley FA Cup Final in 1970?
3. When were the first Winter Olympics held?
4. Which was the first British soccer team to win the European Cup?
5. On which horse did Lester Piggott first win the Derby?
6. In which year did Daley Thompson first win the Olympic Decathlon?
7. Who was the first woman to take part in the University Boat Race?
8. Who was the first footballer to be knighted?
9. Who were the first people to climb Mount Everest?
10. Who was the first Russian tennis player to take part in a Wimbledon singles final?

What Game?

1. Is played at Stradey Park?
2. Is played at Cowdray Park?
3. Has a player called a hooker?
4. Was called sphairistike in the 1870s?
5. Did Michael Tredgett represent England in 133 times in the 1970s and 1980s?
6. Is also called indoor baseball?
7. Did the Australian Rodney Marsh play?
8. Does his brother Graham Marsh play?
9. Do the Los Angeles Dodgers play?
10. Does Tony Cottee play?

———

They're In Charge

Do you know the names of the bodies that govern the following sports in Great Britain?

1. Horse racing (on the flat).
2. Motor racing.
3. Cricket.
4. Football (soccer).
5. Rugby.
6. Jogging.
7. Tennis.
8. Skating.
9. Rowing.
10. Gymnastics.

Famous Faces

Can you identify the sportsmen and women pictured here and say what their sports are? To help you, here is a list of the sports they are associated with:
Three-day eventing, darts, snooker, swimming, skating, squash, motor racing, boxing, athletics, shooting.

1

2

3

4

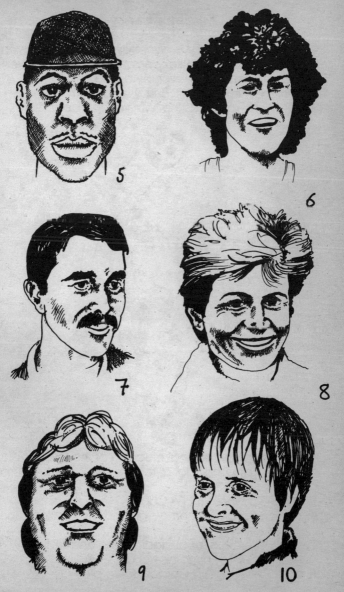

Football Crazy

1. Now a famous TV personality, he was once an accomplished goalkeeper, and Nottingham Forest wanted him as a player. Who is he?
2. Which team did Matt Busby manage?
3. Who was known as the 'Wizard of Dribble'?

4. What was the original meaning of the word 'Wanderers' attached to a team's name, e.g. Bolton Wanderers?
5. Who won the 1989 FA Cup?
6. Which team's home ground is called the Hawthorns?
7. Who scored a goal against England in the 1986 World Cup by using his hand?
8. What position did Gordon Banks play?

9. Up to the end of the 1987–88 Football League season, only three teams had won the Championship in the 1980s. Aston Villa was one. Who were the other two?

10. Formed in 1889, this Yorkshire team has used the same ground for a hundred years. They last won the FA Cup in 1925, with a one–nil win over Cardiff City. Who are they?

Sports Allsorts
1

1. In which sport does Gert Fredriksson hold six Olympic gold medals?

2. What might be Cumberland and Westmorland, Graeco-Roman, or Devon and Cornwall?

3. In which sport is there a puissance event?

4. Who is the only cricketer to score over 10,000 runs in Test matches?

5. Put these boxing weights in order, starting with the heaviest: bantamweight, featherweight, welterweight, flyweight.

6. Where is the Dutch Grand Prix (motor racing) held?

7. He won five Olympic gold medals, was the first man to swim 100 metres in less than a minute, and became a famous Hollywood star. Who was he?

8. How many innings per side are played in a Test match?

9. Where is Brabourne Stadium?

10. Which two former National Hunt jockeys have become famous as thriller writers?

With 'Bat' and Ball

1. Which former world champion snooker player made 'upside-down' glasses famous?
2. What is 'gardening' in cricket?
3. How many players are there in an ice hockey team?
4. What is 'Mr Lu's' game?
5. What used to be called a battledore?
6. Jahangir Khan was British Open and World Champion in the early 1980s – in which sport?
7. How long are the sides of the infield, or 'diamond', in baseball?
8. Which bat and ball game originated as a training exercise for North American Indian warriors?
9. How many players are there on each side in a hurling match?
10. In what bat and ball game can a player make a roquet?

Odd Man Out
1

Which of these American football players is the odd
man out?

Personalities

1. Which member of the Royal Family was once elected Sports Personality of the Year?
2. What do Rod Laver, Roger Taylor and Jimmy Connors have in common?
3. Who lost his job as manager of Oxford United in October 1988?
4. Which American football player is known as the Refrigerator?
5. Who finished first in the 100 metres in the Seoul Olympics but was disqualified after a drugs test?
6. Which of the following drivers was never world champion: Graham Hill, Stirling Moss, Jim Clark, John Surtees?
7. Who is the only woman to have won an Olympic gold medal for Britain in the long jump?
8. Who captained England in *two* Test matches against the West Indies in 1988?
9. What was named after Ulrich Salchow and Axel Paulsen?
10. Which famous racing car manufacturer died in 1988?

How Many?

1. Balls in a cricket over?
2. Players in a rugby union team?
3. Lanes in an Olympic swimming pool?
4. Clubs in a set of golf clubs?
5. Balls does a cannon in billiards involve hitting?

6. Feathers can there be in a shuttlecock?
7. Players in a netball team?
8. Innings in a US professional baseball match?
9. Games in a tennis set?
10. Players in a polo team?

Pitching In

What games are played on these pitches and courts?

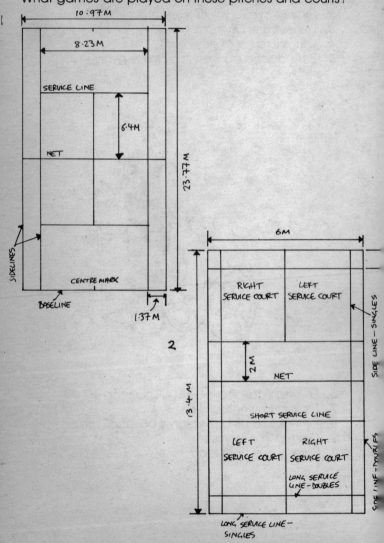

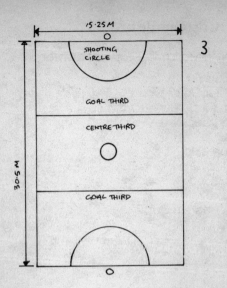

15.25 M

SHOOTING CIRCLE

GOAL THIRD

CENTRE THIRD

GOAL THIRD

30.5 M

3

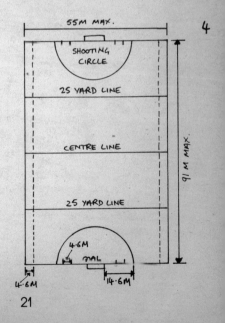

55M MAX.

SHOOTING CIRCLE

25 YARD LINE

CENTRE LINE

25 YARD LINE

GOAL

4.6M

4.6M

14.6M

91 M MAX.

4

Cup Challenge

In which sports are the following trophies awarded?

1. The Stanley Cup?
2. The Westchester Cup?
3. The European Cup-Winners' Cup?
4. The Wightman Cup?
5. The Thomas Cup?
6. The Melbourne Cup?
7. The Queen Elizabeth II Cup?
8. The America's Cup?
9. The Walker Cup?
10. The Benson & Hedges Cup?

Nickname Game

What are the proper names of these football teams?

1. The Shrimpers.
2. The Rams.
3. The Biscuit Men.
4. The Loons.
5. The Cottagers.
6. The Blades.
7. The Minster Men.
8. The Hatters.
9. The Spiders.
10. The Stags.
11. The Bulls.
12. The Sky Blues.
13. The Pirates.

14. The Cherries.
15. The Hammers.

Crossword Challenge

This crossword doesn't have any blanks; the thick black lines indicate where one answer ends and another begins.

Across
1. English football *(6)*
7. Colour awarded for university sport *(4)*
8. The player who bats first in an innings *(6)*
9. An American baseball league *(6)*
11. Something wrong during the football match *(4)*
13. Sebastian Coe once ————— the world record *(5)*
14. Go fast downhill in the snow *(3)*
15. Where the golfer finds the hole *(5)*
16. Football ground with a steep terrace *(3)*
18. Dai ————, a famous golfer *(4)*
20. They help the yachtsman make progress *(5)*
21. Runs very fast (or what you may be in if you lose!) *(5)*
22. It's used by a fisherman *(4)*
23. The Grand ———— is, amongst other things, a rugby competition *(4)*

Down

1. A position on the cricket field *(5)*
2. Caught, bowled, or l.b.w. *(3)*
3. They symbolise membership of a team *(7)*
4. He's in charge of the match *(7)*
5. It's essential for skiers *(4)*
6. The score at 40–40 in tennis *(5)*
7. The All –––––– is a famous rugby team *(6)*
10. The –––––– Crown is both a rugby and a horse-racing title *(6)*
12. Another word for golf course *(5)*
15. Obtains *(4)*
17. It's used to row *(3)*
19. A kind of wrestling for people sitting down *(3)*

Cricket, Lovely Cricket

1. Who was the youngest Englishman ever to play Test cricket?
2. Where, in London, are a) Lord's and b) The Oval?
3. What is an umpire indicating when he raises both arms above his head?
4. What is a 'sticky wicket'?
5. How did the Ashes get their name?
6. Of which team is Phil Neale captain?
7. What is the maximum length of a cricket bat?
8. How long is a bowling crease?
9. Which animal had an obituary notice in *Wisden's Cricketers' Almanack*?
10. Which team has won the County Championship the greatest number of times?

Olympic Games

1. When were the Olympic Games last held in London?
2. Who holds the greatest number of Olympic medals?
3. What do the Olympic rings represent, and what colours are they?

4. Which Olympics were marred by the shooting of eleven Israeli athletes?
5. In the 1980 games there was great rivalry between Steve Ovett and Sebastian Coe. Each won a gold medal, in the 800 and 1500 metres. Who won which medal?
6. When did boxers competing in the Olympics first wear headguards?
7. Which black athlete was 'king' of the 1936 Olympics?
8. What was the name of the 1988 Olympics mascot?
9. What amazing distinction did gymnast Nadia Comaneci obtain in the Montreal Olympics?
10. Which great (and originally barefoot) marathon runner caused a sensation at the Rome Olympics?

Sports Allsorts
2

1. In which game might you make a 'maul pass'?
2. What terrible disaster befell football in 1958?
3. Who captained England's cricket team in the summer series against Australia in 1989?
4. Which game, related to hockey, is a native of Ireland?
5. Under which two bridges do the crews in the University Boat Race pass?

6. What connects St Moritz, Cortina, Cervinia, Königsee, Winterberg, Igls, Sinaia and Lake Placid?
7. Where was the first-ever Test match held?
8. What is the oldest sculling race in the world?
9. Do you recognise this football team whose letters have got muddled up? RACE REX AND E. LAW
10. Who was only seventeen when he competed in the Association Football World Cup Finals for Northern Ireland for 1982?

Initially Speaking

Do you know which sporting associations the following initials stand for?

1. AAA
2. ABA
3. BBBC
4. BSJA
5. FA
6. FEI
7. FIH
8. IFWHA
9. ISRF
10. ITTF
11. LTA
12. MCC
13. NFL
14. NRA
15. RFU

On the Track

How many differences can you spot between these two motor-racing scenes?

Who?

1. Is said to be the person who invented rugby?
2. Won the Olympic tennis men's singles in 1988?
3. Is the only person to have won the Badminton Horse Trials six times?
4. Was World Champion Racing Driver in 1985 and 1986?
5. Scored the only goal of the 1985 FA Cup Final?
6. Were the two gold-medal-winning athletes featured in the film *Chariots of Fire*?
7. Was the only competitor in the 1976 Olympics not to undergo a sex test?
8. Won five World Championships in springboard and highboard diving for the USA in 1978, 1982 and 1986?
9. Was appointed Chairman of the England Selection Committee of the Test and County Cricket Board in March 1989?
10. Partnered Jo Durie to win the Wimbledon mixed doubles title for Britain in 1987?

The Sport of Kings

1. Where is the Derby run?
2. The Derby, Oaks, St Leger, 1000 Guineas and 2000 Guineas are collectively known as – what?
3. What is distinctive about the Oaks and the 1000 Guineas?
4. How long is the Grand National course?
5. Who is the only horse to have won the Grand National three times?
6. This favourite horse and rider won eight consecutive races, including the 1989 Cheltenham Gold Cup, until they fell in the Martell Chase at Aintree in April 1989. Who are they?

7. The 1981 Derby winner was kidnapped. What was his name?

8. What was the name of the great 1930s horse which won the Cheltenham Gold Cup in five consecutive years?

9. Which distinguished jockey partnered Cnoc Na Cuille to victory at Worcester in September 1987?

10. Where is the Cesarewitch run?

One Out of Three

You have a one out of three chance of getting these questions right.

1. In which sport is this glove used?
   a) Cricket?
   b) Baseball?
   c) Rounders?

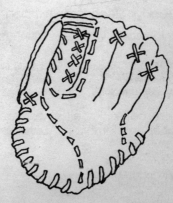

2. In which sport is Tony Allcock a world champion?
 a) Snooker?
 b) Darts?
 c) Bowls?

3. Where was the British Grand Prix (motor racing) held in 1987 and 1988?
 a) Silverstone?
 b) Brands Hatch?
 c) Donington Park?

4. Which pop star raced a yacht called *Drum*?
 a) Paul McCartney?
 b) Simon Le Bon?
 c) George Michael?

5. What was notable about the 1980 women's singles final at Wimbledon?
 a) It was the first to be won on a tie-break?
 b) It was the first to be played at night under floodlights, due to bad weather?
 c) It was the first that Chris Evert won?

6. Who performed the double of 1000 first-class runs and 100 first-class wickets in the 1988 cricket season?
 a) Harvey Trump (Somerset)?
 b) Ian Greig (Surrey)?
 c) Franklyn Stephenson (Nottinghamshire)?

7. In which sport was Cao Yanhua a world champion?
 a) Table tennis?
 b) Squash?
 c) Weight-lifting?

8. A horse called Priceless won the world three-day event championship in Australia in 1986. Who rode it?
 a) Mark Todd?
 b) Virginia Leng?
 c) Lucinda Green?

34

9. Where was Liverpool goalkeeper Bruce Grobbelaar born?
   a) South Africa?
   b) Namibia?
   c) The Netherlands?

10. At which London sports ground can this weathervane be seen?
   a) Lord's cricket ground?
   b) Wembley Stadium?
   c) Wimbledon All-England Tennis Club?

Sporting Language

1. Where, and what, in football is the penalty area?
2. What, in tennis, is a volley?
3. What, in darts, is the inner?
4. What, in baseball, is a fly out?
5. What, in golf, is a birdie?
6. What, in cricket, is a stone waller?
7. What, in motor sport, is going agricultural?
8. Where, in rugby, does the ball go if it goes into touch?
9. What, in horse racing, is a stayer?
10. What, in American football, is the gridiron?

Parade of Champions

1. Who was the first British boxing champion to win three Lonsdale belts outright?

2. Whom did Boris Becker beat in the 1985 and 1986 Wimbledon men's singles championships?
3. Which female Olympic gymnastics champion won gold medals in the 1976 Games for individual combined exercises, asymmetrical bars and balance beam events?
4. A motor racing champion was badly burned in a crash in 1976, but returned to become world champion again. Who is he?
5. Who is the only golfer to have won each of the four major professional championships twice and the US Amateur?
6. Who won his sixth world snooker championship with great ease in 1989?
7. Koichi Nakano has won a record number of world titles. In which sport?
8. Who beat Wigan 32–18 at Naughton Park in April 1989 to retain the Stones Bitter Championship?
9. What did a horse called Charisma achieve in the 1984 and 1988 Olympics?
10. Who won Olympic gold medals in the women's 100 metres freestyle swimming in 1956, 1960 and 1964?

Quite Batty

What sport is each of these 'bats' associated with?

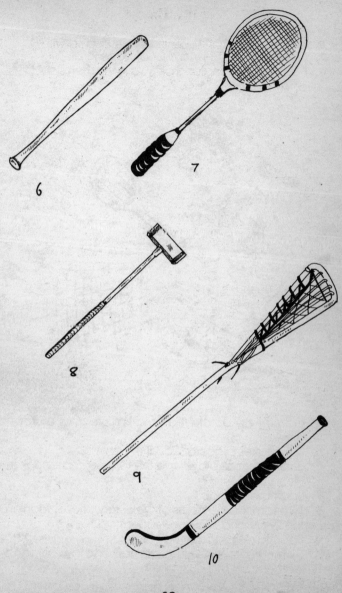

6

7

8

9

10

Which?

1. Sport is governed by the Queensberry Rules?
2. Crew won the University Boat Race in 1989?
3. Future king of England played in the men's doubles at Wimbledon in 1926?

4. Game may be played on a flat green or a crown green?
5. Sport takes place at Royal Birkdale?
6. Bristol football player ate the referee's notebook in December 1983?
7. Sport uses a 'bob'?
8. Two famous members of the Surrey cricket team in the 1940s and 1950s were identical twins?
9. Sport takes place at Burghley?
10. Game is played with a caman and a wool- and leather-covered cork ball?

Sports Allsorts
3

1. Who won the 1989 London Marathon?
2. Where is Trent Bridge?
3. Who are the five nations who play in the Five Nations Rugby Championships?
4. What sport, apart from skiing, takes place on a piste?
5. Who is the only person to have been both World Champion Racing Driver and Motor Cyclist?
6. As whom did tennis player Miss B. J. Moffatt become better known?
7. Who or what is Ballyregan Bob?
8. Where does good play on the green win a green jacket?
9. On 13 April 1936 football player Joe Payne of Luton Town set a record which still stands. What was it?
10. Who won the 1989 *Women's* University Boat Race?

Sports Search

The twenty-one sports and games listed below are hidden in the grid. The names may be read across, down or diagonally, either forwards or backwards, but they are always in straight lines. When you've found them all, see if you can link the two faces in the centre with two of them.

ARCHERY
ATHLETICS
BADMINTON
CRICKET
CROQUET
CYCLING
FOOTBALL

GYMNASTICS
HANG GLIDING
HOCKEY
JUDO
NETBALL
ORIENTEERING
ROWING

RUGBY
SAILING
SKATING
SQUASH
SWIMMING
TENNIS
WATER SKIING

```
W  R  I  B  L  T  S  C  I  T  S  A  N  M  Y  G
A  E  T  G  E  L  L  A  B  T  O  O  F  B  R  N
T  R  O  N  G  C  R  O  Q  U  E  T  G  S  E  I
E  P  N  I  G  T           X  U  N  A  H  D
R  I  S  L  N  E           R  P  I  I  C  I
S  C  A  C  I  O           P  T  M  L  R  L
K  B  C  Y  R  T           F  O  M  I  A  G
I  L  N  C  E  S           A  L  I  N  G  G
I  D  V  O  E  K           T  E  W  G  O  N
N  P  C  L  T  Y           H  Q  S  N  T  A
G  H  R  L  N  E           L  I  M  I  C  H
A  T  I  A  E  K           E  L  V  T  S  W
B  J  C  B  I  C           T  H  J  A  N  R
T  U  K  T  R  O  W  I  N  G  I  M  U  K  L  L
E  D  E  E  O  H  N  H  L  O  C  Q  U  S  B  E
N  O  T  N  I  M  D  A  B  A  S  A  B  R  T  O
```

42

Record Breakers

1. Which swimmer won seven Olympic gold medals at the Munich Olympics in 1972?
2. Who set a world marathon record in 1988?
3. Which king of motor racing won the World Drivers' Championship five times in the 1950s?
4. Who set Olympic records in the 1984 Olympics in the women's 200 metres and 400 metres?
5. Who is the only tennis player to have won two Grand Slams?
6. Which horse set a record time for winning the Derby in 1936?
7. In motor cycle racing, who was the first man to win the 250 cc and the 500 cc in the same year?
8. Who set an Olympic record throwing the javelin in the 1984 Games?
9. What is the fastest anyone has ever swum the English Channel?
10. Who was the youngest player ever to win a match at Wimbledon?

County Badges

Which county cricket clubs do these badges belong to?

1

2

3

4

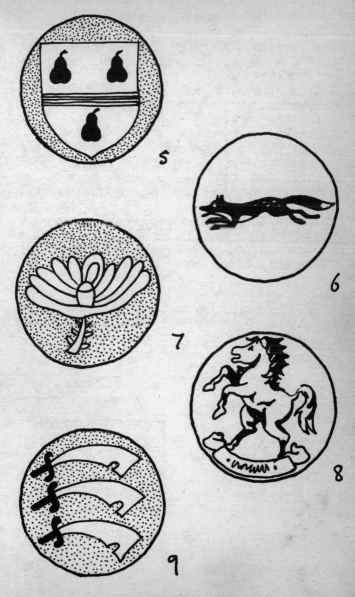

5

6

7

8

9

Rules and Regulations

1. When do players change ends in a tennis match?
2. Who, in a game of association football, is allowed to handle the ball?
3. What is a bye in cricket?
4. What happens if you strike the cue ball directly into a pocket in snooker?
5. How long are the intervals in a game of netball?
6. Can a hockey player stop the ball with his or her hands?
7. Can a basketball player run with the ball?
8. Who can make a forward pass in American football?
9. What must karate and judo contestants wear on their feet?
10. What did figure skaters begin their competitions with until 31 March 1990?

What's in a Name?

1. Which football team is known as Bully Wee?
2. Which great Olympic runner was known as the Clockwork Czech?
3. What is the *maillot jaune*, and who wears it?
4. How is Edson Arantes do Nascimento better known?
5. What is a Fosbury Flop?

6. Which motor race is known as the race of a thousand corners?
7. Which boxer was known as Our 'Enery?
8. Who was known as Little Mo?
9. The name of Dr W. G. Grace is synonymous with cricket. What did his initials stand for?
10. What was tennis player Evonne Cawley's maiden name?

Gym'll Fix It

What are these pieces of gymnastics equipment called?

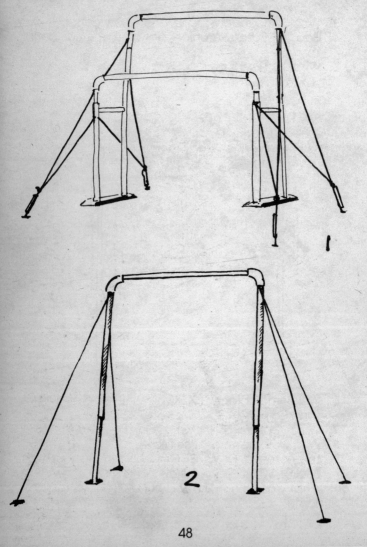

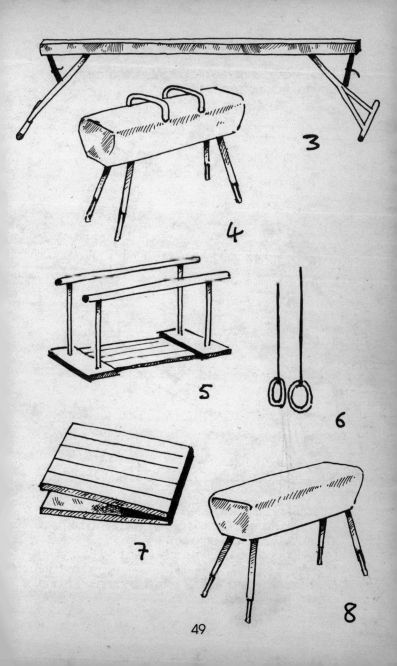

3

4

5

6

7

8

True or False?

1. In the early nineteenth century, cricket bats were curved. True or false?

2. Funso Banjo is a table tennis player. True or false?
3. The 1992 Olympic Games are scheduled to be held in Birmingham. True or false?
4. Lester Piggott won his first race when he was twelve. True or false?
5. Fred Davis was a former world champion tennis player. True or false?

6. Dennis Lillee batted in a 1979 Test match with an aluminium bat. True or false?
7. The BBC TV programme *Grandstand* celebrated fifty years of broadcasting in 1988. True or false?
8. Major Ernst Killander invented orienteering in 1918. True or false?
9. The Uber Cup is awarded for swimming. True or false?
10. Reinhold Messner is the first person in the world to have climbed the fourteen mountains in the world over 8000 metres high. True or false?

Where?

1. Is Old Trafford?
2. Does the pitcher stand in a baseball game?
3. Is the St Leger usually run?
4. Were the Women's World Team Squash Championships held in 1989?
5. Would you begin play with your ball on a baulk line?
6. Is the Derby Bank?
7. Were the 1988 Winter Olympics held?
8. Might you see 'hash marks'?
9. Is a bend called the Station Hairpin?
10. Would you see a cushion, a pocket, a head string and a rack?

On the Wing

Eight of the feathered friends below are nicknames of British football teams; two are not. Can you identify the football teams, and say what the other two are?

1. Swans.
2. Robins.
3. Kiwis.
4. Bluebirds.
5. Magpies.
6. Canaries.
7. Peacocks.
8. Chanticleers.
9. Gulls.
10. Owls.

All England in South-west London

1. When were the All-England tennis championships first held at Wimbledon?
2. Who was the youngest-ever Wimbledon champion?
3. How many times did Bjorn Borg win the men's singles title between 1975 and 1982?
4. Who won the women's singles finals in 1982, 1983, 1984, 1985, 1986 and 1987?
5. Who won the women's singles championship in 1988?
6. Ivan Lendl's coach was a former Wimbledon doubles champion. What is his name?
7. What record did Helen Wills-Moody set between 1927 and 1933?
8. For which country did Maria Bueno play?
9. Which Wimbledon champion underwent open-heart surgery?
10. Fred Perry was the men's singles champion for three years running. When?

Sports Venues

The places listed below are all shown on the map. Each is associated with a particular sport. Can you identify each place, and say with which sport it is associated?

Aintree
Badminton
Bramall Lane
Brands Hatch
Cardiff Arms Park
Hampden Park
Henley
Hickstead
St Andrews
Silverstone
Twickenham
Wembley

Native Lands

Where do the following sportsmen and women come from?

1. Kenny Dalglish.
2. Martine Le Moignan.
3. Kapil Dev.
4. Jack Nicklaus.
5. Edwin Moses.
6. Sue Pountain.
7. Doug Mountjoy.
8. Steve Cram.
9. Steve Cauthen.
10. Yiannis Kouros.
11. Ilie Nastase.
12. Vivian Richards.
13. Martina Navratilova.
14. Pat Cash.
15. Hannu Mikkola.
16. He Zhili.
17. Ecaterina Szabo.
18. Astrid Strauss.
19. Imran Khan.
20. Betty Stove.

What on Earth?

Can you recognise these strange-looking objects, and do you know which sports they are used in?

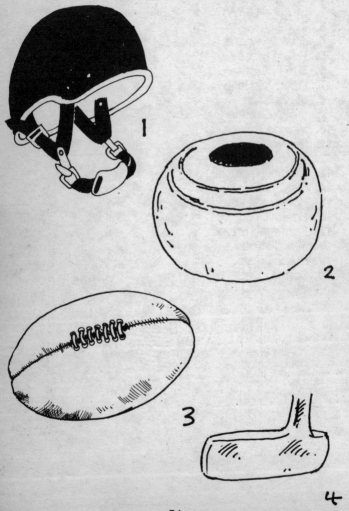

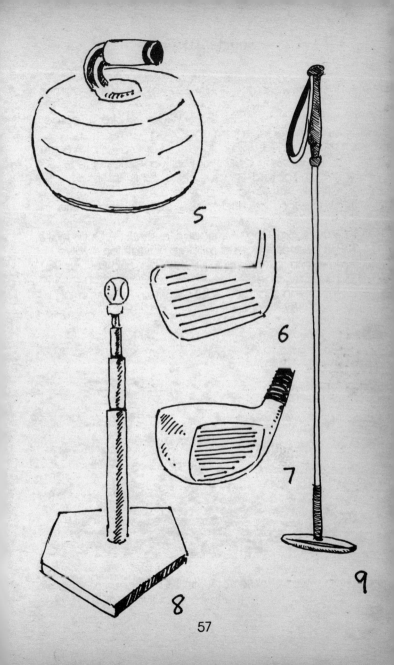

5

6

7

8

9

Sports Allsorts
4

1. Where were the 1986 Commonwealth Games held?
2. What connects Be Fair, Wide Awake, George, Killaire, Regal Realm and Beagle Bay?
3. Which world champion snooker player played in the European Open with his leg in plaster in 1989?
4. Which Football League clubs did TV sports personality Jimmy Greaves play for?
5. Who won the US Masters golf championship in 1989?
6. Who scored the only goal in the 1988 FA Cup Final?
7. What events does a modern pentathlon involve?
8. In which sport were the Schneider and Pulitzer Trophies awarded?
9. Who won a gold medal for Britain for swimming in the 1988 Olympics?

10. Who won the Senior World Cross-country Championships for the fourth consecutive year in 1989?

Playing at Home

Match the home grounds on the left with the soccer teams on the right.

1.	Anfield Road	*a*	Ipswich Town
2.	Annfield Park	*b*	Coventry City
3.	White Hart Lane	*c*	Sheffield Wednesday
4.	Ibrox Stadium	*d*	Scunthorpe United
5.	Valley Parade	*e*	Tottenham Hotspur
6.	Old Trafford	*f*	Stirling Albion
7.	Goodison Park	*g*	Wolverhampton
8.	Portman Road		Wanderers
9.	The Dell	*h*	Luton Town
10.	Dens Park	*i*	Mansfield Town
11.	Highfield Road	*j*	Liverpool
12.	Ashton Gate	*k*	Arsenal
13.	Field Mill	*l*	Everton
14.	Highbury	*m*	Sunderland
15.	Roker Park	*n*	Rangers
16.	Fratton Park	*o*	Dundee
17.	Old Show Ground	*p*	Bristol City
18.	Loftus Road	*q*	Manchester United
19.	Molineux	*r*	Southampton
20.	Hillsborough	*s*	Portsmouth
21.	Kenilworth Road	*t*	Queen's Park Rangers
		u	Bradford City

Uncle Sam's Game

Do you know what these American football signals mean?

Weights and Measures

1. How big is a full-sized table tennis table?
2. In cricket, how far apart are the bowling crease and the popping crease?
3. In amateur boxing, how heavy is a heavyweight?
4. In athletics, how long does a race have to be before a runner may be given refreshments?
5. How long is a rounders bat?
6. How tall is a netball goalpost?
7. How heavy are the shots that a) men, and b) women, put?
8. How far from the floor is the cut, or service line, on a squash court?
9. How long is the hand-over zone in a relay race?
10. How heavy may the ball used in tenpin bowling be?

What?

1. Is the maximum width a cricket bat may be?

2. Does a white belt in karate signify?
3. Is a punt in rugby?
4. In English horse racing, is the Triple Crown?
5. Have Billy Wright and Bobby Moore in common?
6. Colour are the lines on the floor of a squash court?
7. Happens at Le Mans, in France, in June?
8. Game uses a puck?
9. Are the two main categories of competitive skiing called?
10. Does hitting the bullseye score in darts?

Not Many People Know This

1. Which game, known as the 'roaring game', involves energetic sweeping of the course with brooms?
2. Where is the Welsh Grand National run?
3. Which baseball player was known as 'The Georgia Peach'?
4. Who is the only cricket player to take over 300 first-class wickets in an English season?
5. Vasili Alexeyev broke eighty world records in the 1970s. Doing what?
6. Why did Eddie 'the Eagle' Edwards become famous?
7. What is the difference between rowing and sculling?
8. Which Test cricketer had the same initials as the MCC?
9. Which English game does the French *pétanque* or *boule* resemble?
10. In 1960 Brian Phelps won an Olympic bronze medal for Britain. What for?

Crazy Golf

This golfer isn't very good! He has hit the balls into all kinds of strange places! How many can you spot in the picture?

Football International

The strange words and phrases below are made from the muddled-up names of ten foreign football players. Can you unscramble the words and name the players?

1. ADIE AND GROOM A.
2. VINE OR GOAL B.
3. CRUNN OFF JAY H.
4. RARE VALE SAID OF BRUISE I.E.
5. MILK GRAZE RUIN GEM HEN.
6. NAZE BACK FUR BEN E.R.
7. INK GLOB HOLE.
8. PLAIT LIME CHIN.
9. ANN STAB MAC OVER.
10. OASIS POLO R.

Sports Allsorts
5

1. Which club took a stand against football violence by banning away fans at matches?
2. Who would compete in the Paris–Roubaix Classic?
3. What is real tennis?
4. Where in Britain does the General Portfolio road race take place?
5. What is Johnny Herbert's sport?
6. She ran in the Olympic Games, won two world cross-country titles and broke the 5000 metres world record, yet caused a political storm and in 1988 had to leave Britain. Who is she?

7. Where are the 1991 World Student Games to be held?
8. The father is manager of Nottingham Forest football team, the son plays for them. Who are they?
9. Who was the jockey who overcame cancer to win the 1981 Grand National?
10. Who won 122 400-metre hurdle races in succession between 1977 and 1987?

Clear Round

1. Show-jumping fences have a flag on each side, one red and one white, to indicate in which direction they are to be jumped. Which flag is on which side?
2. Who won the European Championship in 1981, 1983 and 1985?
3. How many faults are incurred in show jumping for
   a) knocking down a fence?
   b) refusing a fence?
   c) a fall of horse or rider?

4. Which horse, partnered by John Whitaker, was famous for his kick-back after completing a round?
5. Which popular show-jumping father has two sons who are also successful in the sport?
6. Who is the only horse to have won both the King George V Gold Cup and the Queen Elizabeth II Cup?
7. Who holds the British record for the highest fence jumped?
8. What was the name of the 14.2 hh pony on which Marion (Coakes) Mould won a silver medal in the 1968 Mexico Olympics?
9. Who were the great Italian show-jumping brothers whose horses included The Rock and Gowran Girl?
10. Which famous British horse did *not* go to the Seoul Olympics, though he was Invited to do so?

Top Trophies

Can you identify the trophies pictured here? Two are football trophies, one cricket, two golf and three are tennis.

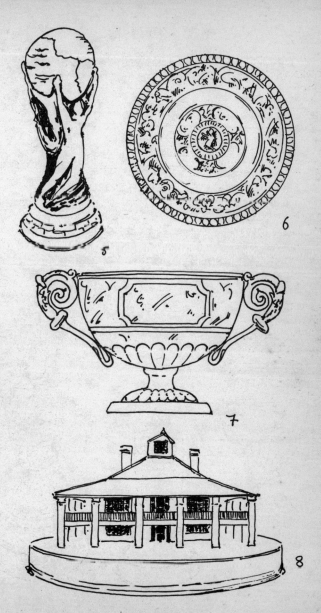

5

6

7

8

Mix 'n' Match

Match the players on the left with the sports on the right.

1.	Martin Bell	*a*	cricket
2.	Steve Cauthen	*b*	football
3.	David Gower	*c*	running
4.	Kevin Keegan	*d*	show jumping
5.	Annette Lewis	*e*	skiing
6.	Hana Mandlikova	*f*	swimming
7.	Nigel Mansell	*g*	golf
8.	Liz McColgan	*h*	horse racing
9.	Adrian Moorhouse	*i*	boxing
10.	Peter Oosterhuis	*j*	javelin throwing
11.	Barry Sheene	*k*	ice skating
12.	Steve Smith	*l*	tennis
13.	Fatima Whitbread	*m*	motor racing
14.	Howard Winstone	*n*	motor cycle racing
15.	Katarina Witt	*o*	rugby

Scoring Points

1. What is the score for potting the blue ball in snooker?
2. How many points does a touchdown score in American football?
3. How long does a bout in fencing last?
4. How is the scoring done in a three-day event?
5. What is the 'game' score in a women's singles badminton match?
6. What is the lowest possible finishing score in darts?
7. How does a baseball player score a home run?
8. What constitutes a count out (knockout) in boxing?
9. Who, in an ice-hockey game, is awarded points known as 'assists'?
10. In the diagram, how many points are scored for a hit in each of the marked areas of the archery target?

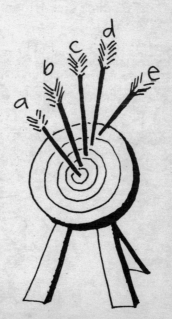

Stumped!

1. Where is Edgbaston cricket ground?
2. Which county did Geoff Boycott play for?
3. How many first-class county cricket teams are there in Great Britain?
4. Who, in Swansea in 1968, hit six sixes in one over?
5. Who captained the undefeated England women's cricket team from 1966 to 1977?
6. Which county team's home ground is Lord's?
7. What is Dennis Lillee's nationality?
8. What do the following cricket terms mean?
   a) Beamer
   b) Quickie
   c) Duck
   d) Googly
   e) Hat trick
9. What do these umpire's signals mean?

Mystery Personalities

Do you recognise these well-known sporting personalities?

1

2

3

4

5

6

Marathon Men and Women

1. How long is a marathon?
2. When was the London Marathon first run?
3. Who was the fastest woman in the 1989 London Marathon?
4. Who was the 1987 world championship marathon winner?
5. An Ethiopian policeman won the 1989 Rotterdam Marathon. What was his name?
6. In 1984 and 1985, he produced the world's best time over 200 kilometres, 200 miles, 500 kilometres, 500 miles, 1000 kilometres, the 24-hour race, 48-hour race and six-day race. Who is he?
7. Which two Norwegian women have dominated marathon running?
8. Who won the 93rd Boston Marathon?
9. What is the fastest time in which a marathon has been run?
10. She won the women's Vienna Marathon in 1989, and was former holder of the world's best time. Who is she?

What's Their Game?

What game is played by each of the following teams and players?

1. Norman Dagley.
2. Miami Dolphins.
3. Michel Platini.
4. Harlequins.
5. Michael Holding.
6. Philadelphia Warriors.
7. Severiano Ballesteros.
8. Derby County.
9. Jimmy White.
10. New York Yankees.

When?

1. Was the first modern Olympic Games held?
2. Did Virginia Wade win the women's singles title at Wimbledon?
3. Was the first Test Match?
4. Did England win association football's World Cup?
5. Was Muhammad Ali (as Cassius Clay) first world heavyweight boxing champion?
6. Were the Commonwealth Games held in London?
7. Was synchronised swimming first included in the Olympic Games?
8. Did Manchester United last win the FA Cup?
9. Did Torvill and Dean first win the World Ice Dance Championship?
10. Did Matt Biondi set a world record for the 100 metres freestyle swimming race of 48.42 seconds?

What's Wrong?

There are at least ten things wrong with this soccer scene. How many can you spot?

Golden Oldies

Match these former champions on the left with their sport on the right. (NB Some sports are associated with more than one player.)

1.	Giacomo Agostini	*a*	athletics
2.	Sydney Barnes	*b*	baseball
3.	Danny Blanchflower	*c*	boxing
4.	Beryl Burton	*d*	cricket
5.	Joe Davis	*e*	cycling
6.	Herb Elliott	*f*	football
7.	Sonja Henie	*g*	golf
8.	Lew Hoad	*h*	gymnastics
9.	Hashim Khan	*i*	horse racing
10.	Jean-Claude Killy	*j*	ice skating
11.	Olga Korbut	*k*	motor cycle racing
12.	Rod Laver	*l*	motor racing
13.	Anita Lonsborough	*m*	show jumping
14.	Willie Mays	*n*	skiing
15.	Bruce McLaren	*o*	snooker
16.	Arnold Palmer	*p*	squash
17.	Sir Gordon Richards	*q*	swimming
18.	Sugar Ray Robinson	*r*	tennis
19.	Pat Smythe		
20.	Bert Trautmann		

Which of these show jumpers is the odd one out?

Sports Allsorts
6

1. What do 'rough' and 'smooth' signify in tennis?
2. Which school game is played between the Oppidans and the Collegers?
3. Which sport takes place at Bisley?
4. Which famous baseball player was once married to Marilyn Monroe?
5. What sport takes place at The Curragh?
6. If you were taking part in the Kellogg's Tour of Britain, what would you be doing?
7. What connects Tim Hutchings, Gary Staines, Dave Clarke, Eamonn Martin and Dave Lewis?
8. Which woman tennis player's unbeaten 31-match run was brought to an end by Gabriela Sabatini in Florida in 1989?
9. Who held, respectively, the Hi-Tec British Open men's and women's squash titles in 1989?
10. In which sport is the Federation Cup awarded?

In 1989 . . .

1. Which world championships were held in Geel, Belgium, in March?
2. Who won the world table tennis championship?
3. Richmond met Wasps in April for the third consecutive year, and Richmond won for the first time. What was the occasion?
4. Who won the Littlewoods Cup Final?
5. Which 28–1 outsider won the 150th Grand National?
6. Which former men's champion put himself out of Wimbledon with an Achilles' tendon injury in the spring?
7. Who won the Monaco Grand Prix despite losing first and second gears?
8. Where were the Embassy World Professional Snooker Championships held?
9. Which dual Olympic champion almost won the Badminton Horse Trials on a horse he'd ridden for less than a week, but knocked down a fence in the last phase to come third?
10. Where were the European Ice Figure Skating Championships held?

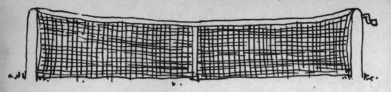

ANSWERS

Firsts, page 9
1. Roger Bannister.
2. The match resulted in a draw and had to be re-played.
3. 1924.
4. Celtic.
5. Never Say Die.
6. 1980.
7. Susan Brown (Oxford cox 1981 and 1982).
8. Stanley Matthews.
9. Edmund Hillary and Tenzing Norgay.
10. Alex Metreveli.

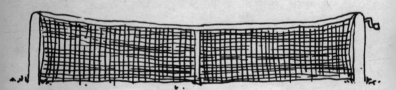

What Game?, page 10
1. Rugby union.
2. Polo.
3. Rugby league and union.
4. Lawn tennis.
5. Badminton.
6. Softball.
7. Cricket.
8. Golf.
9. Baseball.
10. Football.

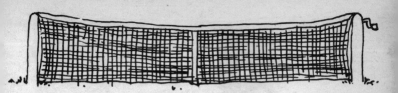

They're in Charge, page 11
1. The Jockey Club.
2. RAC Motor Sports Association.
3. The Test and County Cricket Board.
4. The Football Association.
5. The Rugby Football Union and the Rugby Football League.
6. The National Jogging Association.
7. The Lawn Tennis Association.
8. The National Skating Association of Great Britain.
9. The Amateur Rowing Association.
10. The British Amateur Gymnastics Association.

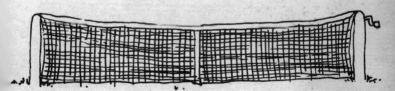

Famous Faces, page 12
1. Malcolm Cooper – shooting.
2. Jayne Torvill – skating.
3. Joe Johnson – snooker.
4. Kornelia Ender – swimming.
5. Frank Bruno – boxing.
6. Kirsty Wade – athletics.
7. Nigel Mansell – motor racing.
8. Virginia Leng – three-day eventing.
9. Eric Bristow – darts.
10. Vicki Cardwell – squash.

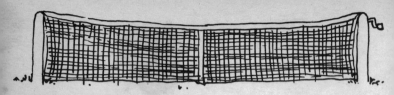

Football Crazy, page 14

1. David Frost.
2. Manchester United.
3. Stanley Matthews.
4. It meant the team had no home ground, and only played away matches.
5. Liverpool.
6. West Bromwich Albion.
7. Diego Maradona.
8. Goalkeeper.
9. Liverpool and Everton.
10. Sheffield United.

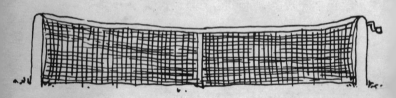

Sports Allsorts 1, page 15

1. Canoe racing.
2. Wrestling.
3. Show jumping.
4. Sunil Gavaskar.
5. Welterweight, featherweight, bantamweight, flyweight.
6. Zandvoort.
7. Johnny Weissmuller.
8. Two.
9. Bombay.
10. Dick Francis and John Francome.

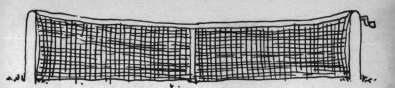

With 'Bat' and Ball, page 16

1. Dennis Taylor.
2. Repairing or flattening part of the pitch damaged by the ball's contact.
3. Six.
4. Golf.
5. A badminton racket.
6. Squash.
7. 27.4 metres (90 feet).
8. Lacrosse.
9. Fifteen.
10. Croquet.

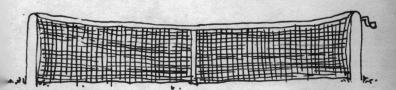

Odd Man Odd 1, page 17

Player number 1 is the odd man out.

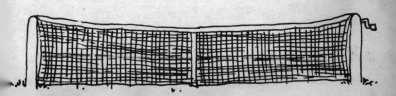

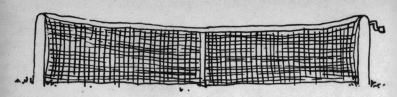

Personalities, page 18

1. The Princess Royal.
2. They are all left-handed tennis players.
3. Mark Lawrenson.
4. William Perry.
5. Ben Johnson.
6. Stirling Moss.
7. Mary Rand (1964).
8. John Emburey.
9. The salchow and axel figure-skating jumps.
10. Enzo Ferrari.

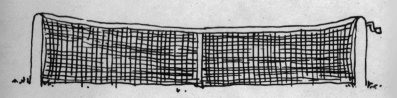

How Many?, page 19

1. Six.
2. Fifteen.
3. Eight.
4. Fourteen.
5. Two, successively.
6. Between fourteen and sixteen.
7. Seven.
8. Nine.
9. At least six. (One player has to win at least six games.)
10. Four.

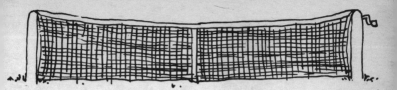

Pitching In, page 20

1. Tennis.
2. Badminton.
3. Netball.
4. Hockey.

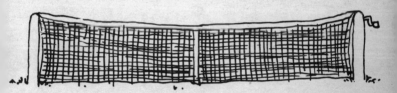

Cup Challenge, page 22

1. Ice hockey.
2. Polo.
3. Association football.
4. Tennis.
5. Badminton.
6. Flat racing.
7. Show jumping (women's).
8. Yachting.
9. Golf.
10. Cricket.

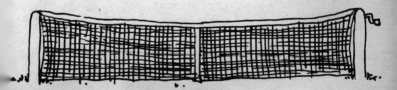

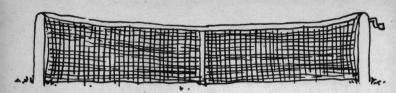

Nickname Game, page 23

1. Southend United.
2. Derby County.
3. Reading.
4. Forfar Athletic.
5. Fulham.
6. Sheffield United.
7. York City.
8. Luton Town.
9. Queens Park.
10. Mansfield Town.
11. Hereford United.
12. Coventry City.
13. Bristol Rovers.
14. Bournemouth.
15. West Ham United.

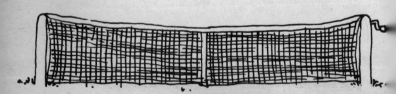

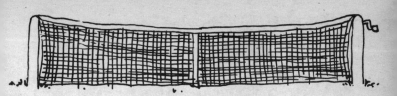

Crossword Challenge, page 24

S	O	C	C	E	R	S	D
B	L	U	E	O	P	E	N	E	R
L	I	T	T	L	E	F	O	U	L
A	P	B	R	O	K	E	W	C	I
C	S	K	I	U	G	R	E	E	N
K	O	P	P	R	E	E	S	A	K
S	A	L	L	S	T	E	A	R	S
R	E	E	L	S	L	A	M

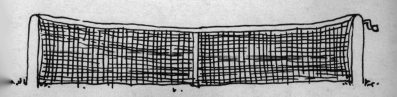

Cricket, Lovely Cricket, page 26

1. Brian Close.
2. St John's Wood (north-west London); Kennington (south-east London).
3. A boundary six.
4. A wet pitch that has begun to dry, forming a hard crust over soft and wet soil.
5. They were supposedly the ashes of a bail burnt after Australia had beaten England in England for the first time in 1882, and the result of a mock obituary notice published in the *Sporting Times*. The ashes were bequeathed to the MCC in 1927.
6. Worcestershire.
7. 38 inches.
8. 8 feet 8 inches.
9. Peter, the Lord's cat (died 5 November 1964 and included in the 1965 edition).
10. Yorkshire.

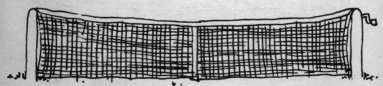

Olympic Games, page 27

1. 1948.
2. Gymnast Larissa Latynina, who holds nine gold, five silver and four bronze medals, which she won during 1956–64.
3. The five continents; (a) blue, (b) yellow, (c) black, (d) green and (e) red.
4. 1972, Munich.
5. Ovett won the 800 metres; Coe the 1500 metres.
6. 1984.
7. Jesse Owens.
8. Hodori, the tiger.
9. She was the first gymnast to be given a perfect score of ten from the judges.
10. Abebe Bikila, who was a complete unknown, and beat many of the world's best runners.

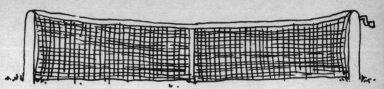

Sports Allsorts 2, page 28

1. Rugby union.
2. The plane carrying Manchester United crashed at Munich, killing eight players.
3. David Gower.
4. Hurling.
5. Hammersmith and Barnes.
6. They all have bobsleigh tracks.
7. Melbourne.
8. Doggett's Coat and Badge on the Thames.
9. Crewe Alexandra.
10. Norman Whiteside.

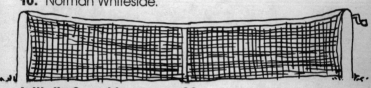

Initially Speaking, page 29

1. Amateur Athletic Association.
2. Amateur Boxing Association.
3. British Boxing Board of Control.
4. British Show Jumping Association.
5. Football Association.
6. Fédération Equestre Internationale.
7. Fédération Internationale de Hockey.
8. International Federation of Women's Hockey Association.
9. International Squash Rackets Federation.
10. International Table Tennis Federation.
11. Lawn Tennis Association.
12. Marylebone Cricket Club.
13. National Football League (American football).
14. National Rifle Association.
15. Rugby Football Union.

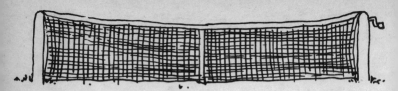

On the Track, page 30

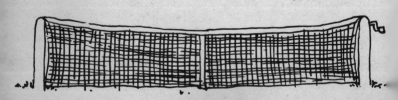

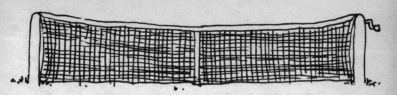

Who?, page 31

1. William Webb Ellis.
2. M. Mecir.
3. Lucinda Green.
4. Alain Prost.
5. Norman Whiteside.
6. Harold Abrahams and Eric Liddell.
7. Princess Anne.
8. Greg Louganis.
9. Ted Dexter.
10. Jeremy Bates.

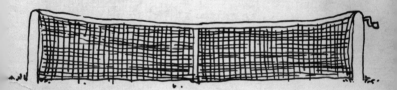

The Sport of Kings, page 32

1. Epsom.
2. The Classic races.
3. They are for fillies only.
4. Approximately four and a half miles.
5. Red Rum.
6. Desert Orchid and Simon Sherwood.
7. Shergar.
8. Golden Miller.
9. The Princess Royal.
10. At Newmarket.

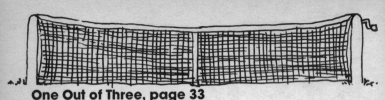

One Out of Three, page 33

1. *b*
2. *c*
3. *a*
4. *b*
5. *a*
6. *c*
7. *a*
8. *b*
9. *a*
10. *a*

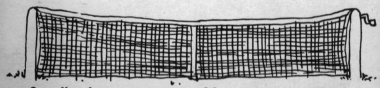

Sporting Language, page 36

1. A rectangle measuring 16.5 metres (18 yards) by 40.3 metres (44 yards) directly in front of the goal.
2. Returning the ball before it reaches the ground and bounces.
3. The small ring round the bullseye in the centre.
4. Getting a player out by catching the ball before it touches the ground.
5. A score of one stroke under par for a hole (par is the score an expert would expect to make. It is governed by the length of the hole).
6. A very defensive batsman, keener on defending the wicket than on making runs.
7. Going off the track or road on to the grass.
8. The ball goes out of play over the sidelines.
9. A horse that can gallop at racing pace over one and a half miles (2.4 kilometres) or further.
10. The football field.

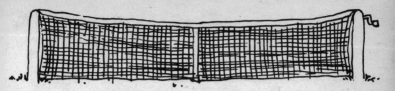

Parade of Champions, page 36

1. Henry Cooper.
2. Kevin Curren and Ivan Lendl.
3. Nadia Comaneci.
4. Niki Lauda.
5. Jack Nicklaus.
6. Steve Davis.
7. Cycling.
8. Widnes.
9. He won the individual gold medal in the three-day event, ridden by Mark Todd.
10. Dawn Fraser.

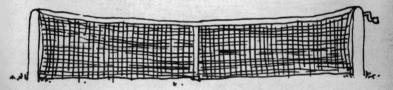

Quite Batty, page 38

1. Cricket.
2. Tennis.
3. Squash.
4. Table tennis.
5. Pelota.
6. Baseball.
7. Badminton.
8. Croquet.
9. Lacrosse.
10. Hockey.

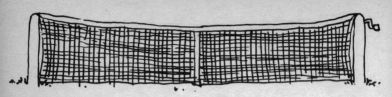

Which?, page 40

1. Boxing.
2. Oxford.
3. George VI.
4. Bowls.
5. Golf.
6. Mike Bagley.
7. Bobsleigh racing.
8. Alec and Eric Bedser.
9. Three-day eventing.
10. Shinty.

Sports Allsorts 3, page 41

1. Douglas Wakiihuri.
2. Nottingham.
3. England, Ireland, Scotland, Wales and France.
4. Fencing.
5. John Surtees.
6. As Billie Jean King.
7. A racing greyhound who holds the record for thirty-two consecutive wins.
8. In the US Masters golf championship at Augusta, Georgia, USA.
9. Scoring ten goals in one Football League match.
10. Cambridge.

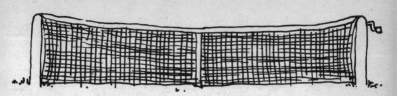

Sports Search, page 42

```
W R I B L T S C I T S A N M Y G
A E T G E L L A B T O O F B R N
T R O N G C R O Q U E T G S E I
E P N I G T X U N A H C D
R I S L N E P I I I C R I
S C A C Y T U R P T M L R G
K B C Y R E F O M I I G
I L N C E S A L I N G N
N I D V O E K T L E W G O A
G P C L T Y H Q S N T C H
A H R I L N E L I M I S W
B J C A B E K T H L V T R L
T U K T R O W I N G I M U K L L
E D E E O H N H L O C Q U S B E
N O T N I M D A B A S A B R T O
```

The faces are those of Linford Christie (athletics) and
Hana Mandlikova (tennis).

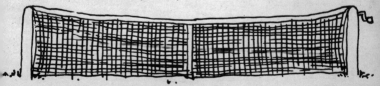

101

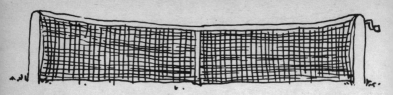

Record Breakers, page 43

1. Mark Spitz.
2. Belayne Dinsamo, 2 hours, 6 minutes, 50 seconds.
3. Juan Fangio.
4. Valerie Brisco-Hooks.
5. Rod Laver.
6. Mahmoud.
7. Freddie Spencer.
8. Tessa Sanderson.
9. Seven hours, forty minutes (1978).
10. Kathy Rinaldi (fourteen years, ninety-one days on 23 June 1981).

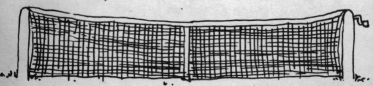

County Badges, page 44

1. Derbyshire.
2. Glamorgan.
3. Northamptonshire.
4. Essex.
5. Worcestershire.
6. Leicestershire.
7. Yorkshire.
8. Kent.
9. Middlesex.

Rules and Regulations, page 46

1. After the first, third, and then every subsequent alternate game of each set, and at the end of each set unless the total number of games in each set is even, in which case the change is not made until the end of the first game of the next set.
2. The goalkeepers.
3. A run scored without the batsman having hit the ball.
4. You lose four points, or the value of the ball on, if it is greater.
5. The first is three minutes, the second ten minutes, the third three minutes.
6. Yes.
7. No, except for dribbling by bouncing the ball while running.
8. The four 'backs' – fullback, quarter-back and two half-backs.
9. Nothing, they have bare feet.
10. A series of 'compulsory figures' based on the figure-of-eight.

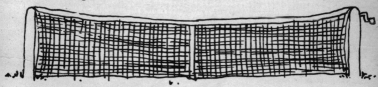

What's in a Name?, page 47

1. Clyde.
2. Emil Zatopek.
3. The yellow jersey; worn by the race leader in the Tour de France cycle race.
4. As Pelé, the great Brazilian football player.
5. A style of high-jumping.
6. The Monaco Grand Prix.
7. Henry Cooper.
8. Maureen Connolly, US tennis player.
9. William Gilbert.
10. Evonne Goolagong.

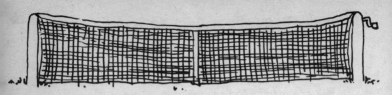

Gym'll Fix It, page 48

1. Asymmetrical bars.
2. Horizontal bar.
3. Beam.
4. Pommel horse.
5. Parallel bars.
6. Rings.
7. Springboard.
8. Vaulting horse.

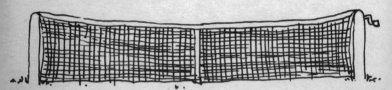

True or False?, page 50

1. True.
2. False, he is a boxer.
3. False, they are scheduled to be held in Barcelona.
4. True.
5. False, he was a former world champion snooker player.
6. True.
7. False, it celebrated thirty years of broadcasting.
8. True.
9. False, it is awarded for badminton.
10. True.

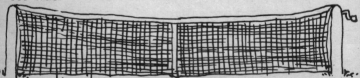

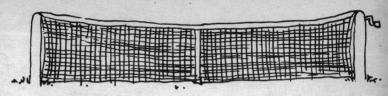

Where?, page 51
1. Manchester.
2. On a mound.
3. Doncaster.
4. Warmond, Netherlands.
5. A croquet lawn, or a billiards or snooker table.
6. Hickstead, Sussex.
7. Calgary, Canada.
8. On an American football pitch.
9. On the Monaco Grand Prix circuit.
10. On a pool table.

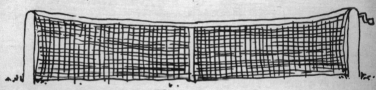

On the Wing, page 52
1. Swansea City.
2. Bristol City or Charlton Athletic.
3. A New Zealand rugby team.
4. Cardiff City.
5. Newcastle United or Notts. County.
6. Norwich City.
7. Leeds United.
8. A French rugby team.
9. Torquay United.
10. Sheffield Wednesday.

All-England in South-west London, page 53
1. 1877.
2. Charlotte (Lottie) Dod, who won in 1877 aged fifteen years and 285 days.
3. Five – 1976 to 1980 inclusive.
4. Martina Navratilova.
5. Steffi Graf.
6. Tony Roche.
7. She did not lose a single set at Wimbledon.
8. Brazil.
9. Arthur Ashe.
10. 1934 to 1936 inclusive.

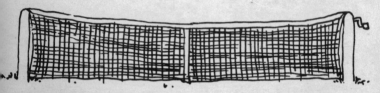

Sports Venues, page 54
1. St Andrews, golf.
2. Hampden Park, football.
3. Aintree, horse racing.
4. Bramall Lane, football and cricket.
5. Cardiff Arms Park, rugby.
6. Silverstone, motor racing.
7. Badminton, three-day event.
8. Henley, rowing.
9. Wembley, football (and other sports).
10. Twickenham, rugby.
11. Hickstead, show jumping.
12. Brands Hatch, motor racing.

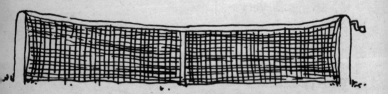

Native Lands, page 55
1. Scotland.
2. Guernsey.
3. India.
4. USA.
5. USA.
6. Great Britain.
7. Wales.
8. Great Britain.
9. USA.
10. Greece.
11. Romania.
12. West Indies.
13. Czechoslovakia.
14. Australia.
15. Finland.
16. China.
17. Romania.
18. German Democratic Republic.
19. Pakistan.
20. Holland.

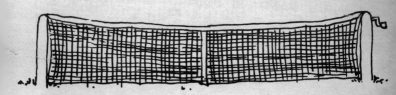

What on Earth?, page 56
1. A jockey's skull cap (horse racing and eventing).
2. A bowl or wood (bowls).
3. A rugby ball.
4. A putter (golf).
5. A curling iron.
6. An iron (golf).
7. A wood (golf).
8. A T-ball tee (baseball, Little League, T-ball).
9. A polo stick.

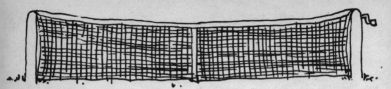

Sports Allsorts 4, page 58
1. Edinburgh.
2. They are the horses on which Lucinda Green won the Badminton Horse Trials.
3. Alex Higgins.
4. Chelsea, Tottenham Hotspur, West Ham United.
5. Nick Faldo.
6. Lawrie Sanchez.
7. Riding an unfamiliar horse, fencing, pistol-shooting, swimming and cross-country running.
8. Flying.
9. Adrian Moorhouse.
10. John Ngugi.

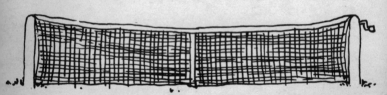

Playing at Home, page 59
1. *j*
2. *f*
3. *e*
4. *n*
5. *u*
6. *q*
7. *l*
8. *a*
9. *r*
10. *o*
11. *b*
12. *p*
13. *i*
14. *k*
15. *m*
16. *s*
17. *d*
18. *t*
19. *g*
20. *c*
21. *h*

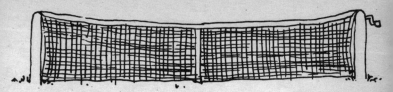

Uncle Sam's Game, page 60

1. Unsportsmanlike conduct (non-contact fouls).
2. Player disqualified.
3. Personal foul.
4. Time out.
5. Touchdown, field goal, or successful try.
6. Dead ball, or neutral zone established.

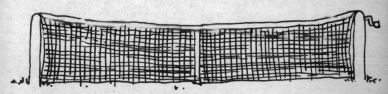

Weights and Measures, page 62

1. 2.74 metres × 1.52 metres (9 ft × 5 ft).
2. 1.22 metres (4 feet).
3. Between 81 kilograms (179 lbs) and 91 kilograms (200 lbs 10 oz).
4. Over 16 kilometres (10 miles).
5. 46 centimetres (18⅜ inches).
6. 3.05 metres (10 feet).
7. 7.26 kilograms (16 lbs) men; 4 kilograms (8 lbs 13 oz) women.
8. 1.83 metres (6 feet).
9. 20 metres (22 yards).
10. Up to 7.25 kilograms (16 lbs).

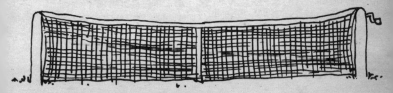

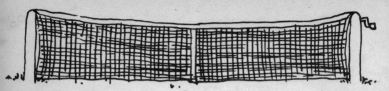

What?, page 63

1. 4¼ inches.
2. A beginner.
3. Letting the ball drop from hand and kicking it before it reaches the ground.
4. The Derby, St Leger and 2000 Guineas.
5. They both captained England ninety times, and both played for England over 100 times.
6. Red.
7. A twenty-four hour motor race.
8. Ice hockey.
9. Nordic and Alpine.
10. Fifty.

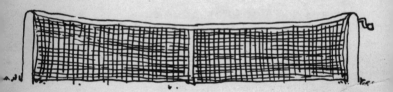

Not Many People Know This, page 64

1. Curling.
2. Chepstow.
3. Ty Cobb.
4. A. P. 'Tich' Freeman in 1928 (304 wickets).
5. Weightlifting.
6. For doing so badly in ski-jumping competitions.
7. Someone rowing pulls one oar; someone sculling pulls two.
8. Michael Colin Cowdrey.
9. Bowls.
10. Diving.

Crazy Golf, page 65
There are 10 golf balls hidden in the picture.

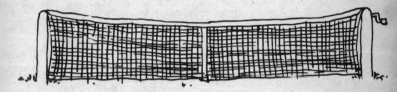

Football International, page 66
1. DIEGO MARADONA.
2. IGOR BELANOV.
3. JOHANN CRUYFF.
4. EUSEBIO FERREIRA DA SILVA.
5. KARL-HEINZ RUMMENIGGE.
6. FRANZ BECKENBAUER.
7. OLEG BLOKHIN.
8. MICHEL PLATINI.
9. MARCO VAN BASTEN.
10. PAOLO ROSSI.

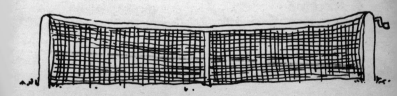

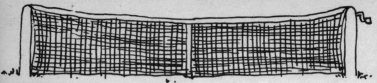

Sports Allsorts 5, page 67

1. Luton Town.
2. A cyclist; it is a cycle race.
3. An indoor racket and ball game dating from the eleventh century. It is still played, though it has been superseded in popularity by lawn tennis.
4. In Newcastle.
5. Motor racing.
6. Zola Budd.
7. In Sheffield.
8. Brian and Nigel Clough.
9. Bob Champion.
10. Ed Moses.

Clear Round, page 68

1. Red on the right; white on the left.
2. Paul Schockemöhle on Deister.
3. *a)* Four faults.
   b) Three faults for the first refusal, six for the second, and elimination for the third.
   c) Eight faults.
4. Ryan's Son.
5. Harvey Smith (Robert and Steven Smith).
6. Sunsalve.
7. Nick Skelton on Lastic (7 ft 7$\frac{5}{16}$ ins – 2.32 metres on 16 December 1978).
8. Stroller.
9. Piero and Raimondo d'Inzeo.
10. Next Milton.

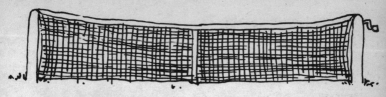

Top Trophies, page 70

1. The FA Cup.
2. The Wimbledon Men's Singles Challenge Cup.
3. The British Open's silver claret jug (golf).
4. The Ashes trophy (cricket).
5. The World Cup (football).
6. The Wimbledon Women's Singles Trophy.
7. The Wimbledon Men's Doubles Trophy.
8. The US Masters trophy (golf).

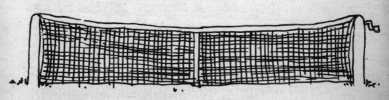

Mix 'n' Match, page 72

1. *e*
2. *h*
3. *a*
4. *b*
5. *d*
6. *l*
7. *m*
8. *c*
9. *f*
10. *g*
11. *n*
12. *o*
13. *j*
14. *i*
15. *k*

Scoring Points, page 73

1. Five points.
2. Six.
3. Until one competitor has scored five hits, with a time limit of six minutes.
4. On a series of penalty points for errors and time faults committed, with bonus points being awarded for completing certain sections in less than the time allowed.
5. Usually eleven.
6. Two (double one).
7. By hitting the ball and running all the way round the infield (i.e. the square formed by the bases) in one turn.
8. A boxer being knocked down and being unable to rise within at least ten seconds, counted by the referee.
9. A player who did not score a goal, but whose play contributed to the scoring of a goal.
10. a) Nine b) Seven c) Five d) Three e) One.

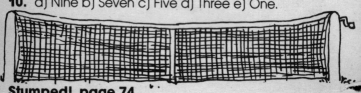

Stumped!, page 74

1. Birmingham.
2. Yorkshire.
3. Seventeen.
4. Gary Sobers.
5. Rachael Heyhoe Flint.
6. Middlesex.
7. Australian.
8. *a)* A fast, head-high, full pitch, classed as unfair play.
   b) A fast bowler.
   c) A score of nought.
   d) An off-break ball bowled with a leg-break action.

    e) A bowler dismissing three batsmen with three consecutive balls.
9. *a)* Out.
    b) Bye.
    c) No ball.
    d) Wide.
    e) Boundary four.
    f) Leg bye.

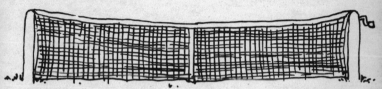

Mystery Personalities, page 76
1. David Gower.
2. Fatima Whitbread.
3. Severiano Ballesteros.
4. Chris Evert.
5. Ian Botham.
6. Tessa Sanderson.

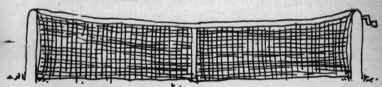

Marathon Men and Women, page 78
1. 26 miles 385 yards (42.195 kilometres).
2. 29 March 1981.
3. Veronique Marot.
4. Douglas Wakiihuri.
5. Belayne Dinsamo.
6. Yiannis Kouros.
7. Grete Waitz and Ingrid Kristiansen.
8. Abebe Mekonnen.
9. Two hours, six minutes, fifty seconds.
10. Christa Vahlensieck.

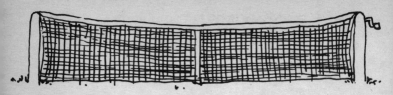

What's Their Game?, page 79

1. Billiards.
2. American football.
3. Football.
4. Rugby Union.
5. Cricket.
6. Basketball.
7. Golf.
8. Football.
9. Snooker.
10. Baseball.

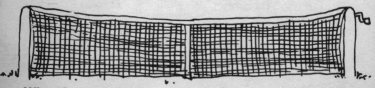

When?, page 80

1. 1896.
2. 1977.
3. 1877.
4. 1966.
5. 1964.
6. 1934.
7. 1984.
8. 1983.
9. 1981.
10. 1988.

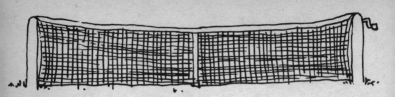

Golden Oldies, page 82

1. k
2. d
3. f
4. e
5. o
6. a
7. j
8. r
9. p
10. n
11. h
12. r
13. q
14. b
15. l
16. g
17. i
18. c
19. m
20. f

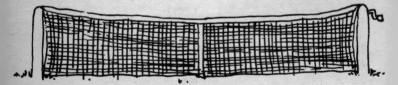

Odd Man Out 2, page 83
Show jumper number 3 is the odd man out.

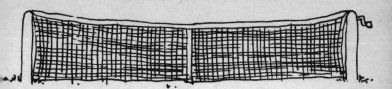

Sports Allsorts 6, page 84

1. They describe two sides of the racket, according to the way it is strung. This description is used when a racket is spun to decide who should serve first in a match and from which end.
2. The Eton wall game.
3. Shooting.
4. Joe di Maggio.
5. Horse racing.
6. Cycling.
7. They were members of Britain's silver-medal-winning cross-country running team in Stavanger, Norway, in March 1989.
8. Steffi Graf's.
9. Jahangir Khan and Susan Devoy respectively.
10. International women's team tennis.

In 1989 . . ., page 85

1. Ice hockey.
2. Jan-Ove Waldner.
3. The Women's Rugby Union Cup Final.
4. Nottingham Forest.
5. Little Polveir.
6. Pat Cash.
7. Ayrton Senna.
8. The Crucible Theatre, Sheffield.
9. Mark Todd.
10. Birmingham.

WORLD CUP 90

PHILIP EVANS

Packed with essential information, *World Cup 90* is the indispensable pocket companion for anyone interested in this year's tournament – whether they will be following the competition on television or actually going to Italy. It includes:

* the Draw for the First Round of matches with relevant map
* an analysis of all the teams competing
* information concerning the leading players
* a special section about Italy, its squad, its grounds and its manager
* two sections of stunning action photographs
* information about the past thirteen tournaments

At home or away, the essential guide to World Cup 90

HODDER AND STOUGHTON

MY MOST EMBARRASSING MOMENT

COMPILED BY COMPLETE EDITIONS

The most embarrassing moments of the famous are brought together in this hilarious collection of true stories from the stars. From Anneka Rice's renowned split trousers to Russell Grant's trousers almost falling down in front of the Queen Mother! Contributions from Esther Rantzen, Rolf Harris, Nicholas Parsons, Michael Aspel – and many, many more.

Royalties to PHAB (Physically Handicapped and Able Bodied) organisation.

HODDER AND STOUGHTON

MY RECORD BOOK

GYLES BRANDRETH

How many pairs of socks can *you* put on, one on top of another?

Can *you* eat an entire tin of baked beans in 19 minutes using only a cocktail stick?

And what exactly are the credentials for being a record-breaker?

Read *My Record Book* and find out!

KNIGHT BOOKS

SOGGY SEMOLINA:
THE SCHOOL DINNERS JOKE BOOK

EGON CHIPS

What's yellow and wobbly and wears dark glasses? What do you get if you cross a hyena with an Oxo cube?

All this and much more is dished up in *The School Dinners Joke Book* (but don't tell the dinner ladies!)

KNIGHT BOOKS